World Series Champions: Chicago Cubs

Second baseman/Outfielder Ben Zobrist

Outfielder Sammy Sosa

WORLD SERIES CHAMPIONS

CHICAGO CUBS

MEGAN COOLEY PETERSON

CREATIVE SPORTS

CREATIVE EDUCATION / CREATIVE PAPERBACKS

Published by Creative Education and Creative Paperbacks
P.O. Box 227, Mankato, Minnesota 56002
Creative Education and Creative Paperbacks are imprints of
The Creative Company
www.thecreativecompany.us

Art Direction by Tom Morgan
Book production by Ciara Beitlich
Edited by Joe Tischler

Photographs by Alamy (Reuters), AP Images (Morry Gash), Getty
(Bettmann, Jonathan Daniel, Focus On Sport, Icon Sportswire,
Scott Kane, Photo File, Michael Reaves, Chris Trotman),
Newscom (Kamil Krzaczynski), Shutterstock (f11photo)

Library of Congress Cataloging-in-Publication Data
Names: Peterson, Megan Cooley, author.
Title: Chicago Cubs / Megan Cooley Peterson.
Description: Mankato, MN : Creative Education and Creative
   Paperbacks, [2024] | Series: Creative sports. World Series
   champions | Includes index. | Audience: Ages 7-10 | Audience:
   Grades 2-3 | Summary: "Elementary-level text and engaging
   sports photos highlight the Chicago Cubs' MLB World Series
   wins and losses, plus sensational players associated with the
   professional baseball team such as Kris Bryant."-- Provided
   by publisher.
Identifiers: LCCN 2023008175 (print) | LCCN 2023008176 (ebook)
   | ISBN 9781640268180 (library binding) | ISBN 9781682773680
   (paperback) | ISBN 9781640009882 (pdf)
Subjects: LCSH: Chicago Cubs (Baseball team)--Juvenile literature.
   | World Series (Baseball)--History--Juvenile literature.
Classification: LCC GV875.C6 P48 2024 (print) | LCC GV875.C6
   (ebook) | DDC 796.357/640977311--dc23/eng/20230223
LC record available at https://lccn.loc.gov/2023008175
LC ebook record available at https://lccn.loc.gov/2023008176

Printed in China

Third baseman Kris Bryant

CONTENTS

Home of the Cubs

The city of Chicago sits next to Lake Michigan in Illinois. It is known as the "Windy City." It is also home to the Chicago Cubs baseball team. The Cubs have played at Wrigley Field since 1916. Green Ivy covers the outfield walls of the **stadium**.

The Cubs are a Major League Baseball (MLB) team. They are in the National League (NL) Central Division. Their **rivals** are the St. Louis Cardinals. All MLB teams try to win the World Series to become champions

Pitcher Fergie Jenkins

Naming the Cubs

In the early days, the Cubs had different names. Among them were White Stockings and Colts. By 1902, the team had many young players. Reporters started calling them "the Cubs." A cub is a young animal. The name stuck. In 1907, the team officially became the Cubs.

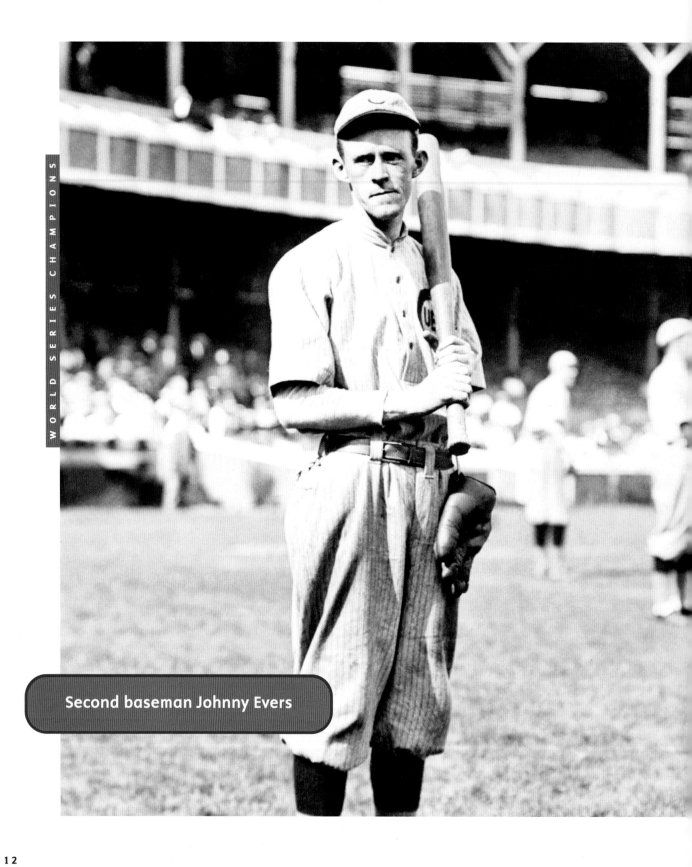

Second baseman Johnny Evers

Cubs History

The Cubs are one of MLB's oldest teams. They joined the NL in 1876. By 1886, they had already won six **pennants**.

In 1907, the Cubs won their first World Series. They beat the Detroit Tigers. The following year, they beat the Tigers again! Second baseman Johnny Evers helped his team become back-to-back champions.

The Cubs returned to the World Series seven times through 1945. They lost all seven series. After that, they had great players such as shortstop Ernie Banks. He was named the NL Most Valuable Player (MVP) in 1958 and 1959. But the Cubs didn't make the playoffs.

Second basemen Ryne Sandberg

Second baseman Ryne Sandberg helped the Cubs make the playoffs in 1984 and 1989. They got there a handful of times after that, too. But the World Series stayed out of reach.

The Cubs' luck changed in the 2016 season. They faced the Cleveland Indians in the World Series. Ben Zobrist drove in the go-ahead run with a hit late in Game 7. For the first time in 108 years, the Cubs were champions!

Other Cubs Stars

Cubs players have always thrilled fans. Star outfielder Billy Williams was one of the league's best hitters. He was named NL **Rookie** of the Year in 1961. Fergie Jenkins was one of the best pitchers in Cubs history. He had more than 2,000 **strikeouts** as a Cub.

Outfielder Billy Williams

Outfielder Ian Happ

Third baseman Kris Bryant joined the team in 2015. He was NL Rookie of the Year in 2015. The next year, he was named NL MVP. Newer players such as Ian Happ and Dansby Swanson are hungry to win. Both players have won Gold Glove awards. The best fielders win it. Fans see another championship in the Cubs' future!

About the Cubs

Started playing: 1870

. . . .

League/division: National
    League, Central Division

. . . .

Team colors: blue, white, and red

. . . .

Home stadium: Wrigley Field

. . . .

WORLD SERIES CHAMPIONSHIPS:

    1907, 4 games to 0 over
    Detroit Tigers

. . . .

    1908, 4 games to 1 over
    Detroit Tigers

. . . .

    2016, 4 games to 3 over
    Cleveland Indians

. . . .

Chicago Cubs website:
    www.mlb.com/cubs

. . . .

Glossary

pennant—a league championship; a team that wins a pennant gets to play in the World Series

....

playoffs—games that the best teams play after a regular season to see who the champion will be

....

rival—a team that plays extra hard against another team

....

rookie—a first-year player

....

stadium—a building with tiers of seats for spectators

....

strikeout—when a batter makes an out by making three strikes in an at-bat

....

Outfielder Seiya Suzuki

Index